BLITZED CHURCH IS REBUILT
The Story of King Street Methodist Church
Pauline Raine

Wednesday, 4th December, 1957. The door of the New King Street Methodist Church being opened by Miss Mabel L. Almond, and dedicated by the Rev. Harold Roberts, President of the Methodist conference for that year.

This version of the book is virtually as originally published, presenting the work of Pauline Raine. There are now additional pages at the back providing information about the publisher, Arthur L Clamp.

The republishing project is being managed by Arthur's grandson, Steven Gibson. We aim to find all the research that he was involved in publishing, preserving it for the next generation as part of 'The Clamp Collection'.

THE STORY OF KING STREET CHURCH

King Street Minister since 1981, Rev. Peter Bolt said:

"Where there is life, there will also be change. This is the fascinating story of the many changes that have taken place since King Street Methodist Church began in 1866. Like most families, the Church has had several homes, so much of the story must be about buildings — especially how the destruction of 1941 became the construction of 1956-57.

But it is also the story of people — God's people. Ordinary people who have a faith, and a vision! People who believe that Jesus is alive, and meet together to work out that faith through worship and service. However, the work is not finished. It will continue so long as the Church which is situated near the main cross-roads of Plymouth, seeks to point the way to pilgrims on the journey of life."

The first King Street Wesleyan Chapel, Plymouth.

New Church in King Street

Back in 1864 they had talked of a 'new' church in King Street. A leading Devonshire Methodist, Mr John Allen of Ivybridge, laid the foundation stone of this new Wesleyan chapel on May 17th, 1864. The 1914 Sunday School Jubilee booklet puts it this way: "The leaders of Methodism in the Plymouth Circuit were men of considerable faith and courage when they decided to build a new church in King Street to seat a congregation of 1,600 and determined that 700 of these sittings should be free." (At that time it was generally accepted practice that a rent should be paid for a pew and in fact many pews in the church bore members' names. This practice has long since been dropped but rents around the twenties and thirties were 2 shillings and 6 pence per quarter, plus 1 penny a week for membership.)

Barley House becomes Available

At that time a new area of Plymouth had become available for building — known as the Barley House Estate; and until then the residence of the Elliot family. The King Street of 1864 was built in this 'new' area, on what we now know as the road between the market and Frankfort Gate (Market Way). The original cost of the building and site was £11,815.

Early Morning Opening

The church was opened in March 1866; the first service being at 7 a.m. when Reverend S. D. Waddy was there to take a prayer meeting for some 700 people. Opening services were then continued for a number of Sundays.

The Cathedral of Western Methodism

King Street chapel was a massive building — a wide frontage, a gable over the centre, three sets of entrance doors and a set of wide approach steps — a building of typical mid-Victorian architecture. It was to become known as the Cathedral of Western Methodism, although the actual head of the circuit was the Ebenezer Chapel, (now the Central Hall) less than half a mile away. Five years after opening it was decided that Ebenezer Circuit was too large for administration and that King Street should be head of another Plymouth Circuit. The 1913 Conference Handbook tells us that there was quite a fight to settle the boundaries of the new circuit. Finally it was decided that the King Street circuit should include besides King Street — Stonehouse, Knackersknowle, Turnchapel, Down Thomas, Tamerton and Oreston, and also a preaching place at Mutley where at the time, services were held in a coach-house or carpenter's shop, 34 feet by 14 feet.

Big Names Come to Preach

Over the years the well-known preachers of the Wesleyan Connexion came to preach there — names such as the Reverends W. L. Watkinson, Hugh Price Hughes, Mark Guy Pearce, Peter Thompson, W. D. Walters, C. Ensor Walters, John H. Goodman, and F. Luke Wiseman. At times other denominations used the chapel, and men such as Reverend J. H. Jowett preached there. It was quite normal to queue for a seat when the 'big names' came, although Miss Gwen Fugler remembered that church members could be sure of their seats by entering the church at the rear in Tracey Street before 5.30 p.m.

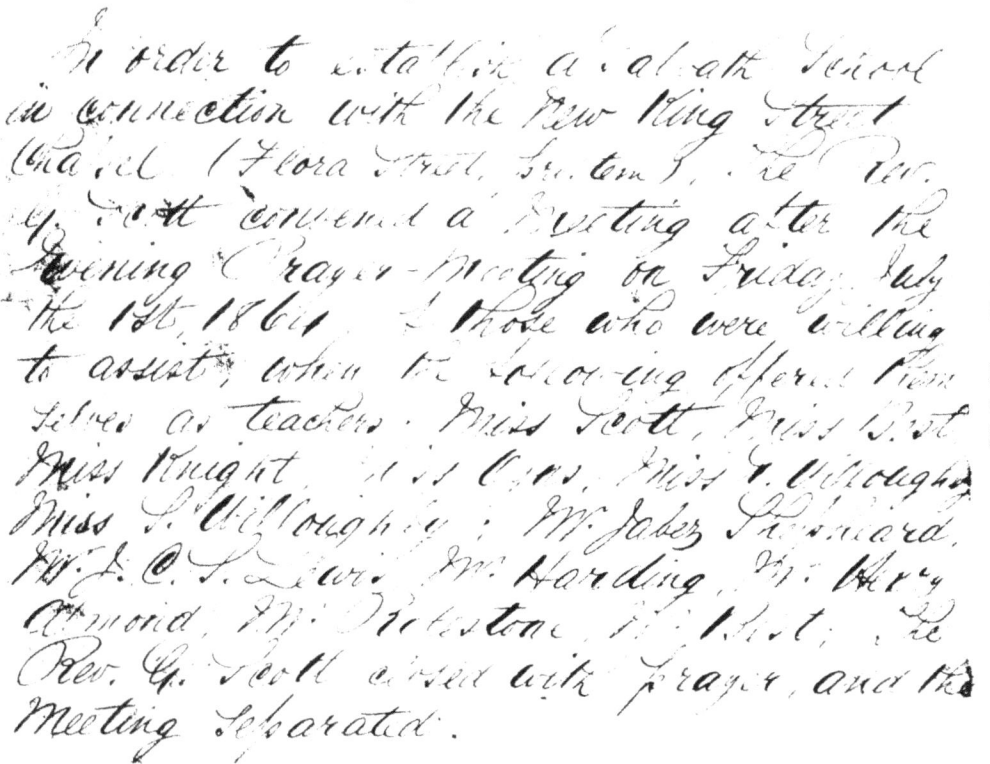

Names of the first Sunday School teachers.

Mr. Jabez Shepheard was the first Superintendent.

Birth of the Sunday School

Although no school premises were included in the original building scheme, land had been acquired for that purpose and on Friday, July 1st, 1864, after an evening prayer meeting the Minister of the Society called together, in a workshop in Flora Street, twelve men and women to establish a Sunday School.

The Flora Street school started on July 3rd, growing so rapidly that by the time the church itself was opened in March 1866, there were 250 children.

The school was transferred to the new church from Flora Street in March, 1866.

Pupils Look Down from Above

In the early days the school was taught in the church with the pupils arranged on each side of the gallery; the organ gallery (minus the organ) being used as a platform with the teachers standing for the lesson while the pupils looked down from above. Separate classes had to be held in vestries; corners under galleries were used, and the Infant class used small forms without backs in the front hallway.

Teachers Pledge Money

Plans for the new School Premises had been formed by 1869, with the teachers pledging to raise £150 towards the cost. In fact they raised £152.12.8d; £37.10.0d being the first instalment by the time of the stone laying in 1870.

The premises of 1870 contained only four classrooms for separate teaching and many references were made at the Sunday School meetings to the need for more. At that time also, an organ was placed in the church.

An extension fund was started in 1884, and in 1894, the Trustees began a major building scheme using the extra ground originally purchased.

KING STREET WESLEYAN CHURCH, PLYMOUTH.

THIS DAY

MEMORIAL STONES of the New Sunday School Building will be placed THIS DAY (WEDNESDAY) OCTOBER 3rd, 1894.

At 1 for 1.30 punctually, Public Luncheon in St. Andrew's Hall. Tickets, 2s. 6d.
At 3.10, a Procession will leave the Hall for the site.
At 3.30, the Ceremony of Stone Laying, Rev. W. Maltby presiding.

The Chief Corner Stone will be laid by
T. OWEN, Esq., M.P.,
And a Trustees' Stone by
MR. J. MAY GROSE.

At 5.30, Tea in the King-street Schoolroom. Tickets, 1s
At 7.0, a Public Meeting in the Chapel.

T. OWEN, Esq., M.P., WILL PRESIDE.

Address by the
REV. C. H. KELLY (of London).

Prior to the unlocking of the doors, however, a portion of that ceremony which was so abruptly ended in October was completed—the declaration that the foundation-stones had been "well and truly laid." Mr. J. M. Grose was responsible for the trustees' stone; and twelve little children performed similar functions in relation to smaller stones on which their initials had been cut. These were—Nellie Hannaford, Lydia S. Cooms, Ethel Davis, Mabel Gaud, Florence Griffin, Olive K. Hosking, Winnifred M. Jolliffe, Gladys Roseveare, Nellie M. Venning, Violet Winnicott, William Spearman, and Victor R. Winnicott.—Rev. W. MALTBY announced with reference to the stone intended to be laid by Mr. T. Owen, M.P., that that gentleman gave a donation of £20 in October, and had promised an additional £10. A silver key was then presented by Mr. Maltby to Miss Green, daughter of the President, who unlocked the new premises amidst applause. A large party inspected the schools, and Rev. WALFORD GREEN, having expressed the pleasure that ceremony had afforded his daughter, the company adjourned to the Lecture Hall.

EVENING MEETING.

The day's proceedings closed with a largely-attended public meeting, the platform being occupied by the President of the Conference (Rev. Walford Green), Rev. F. L. Wiseman, B.A., and the ministers and officers of the circuit. Mr. J. M. GROSE occupied the chair, and in his opening remarks said he was thankful to know that he had seen the desire of his heart in connection with the completion of that building. Referring to the financial position of the enterprise, Mr. Grose reminded the audience that £1,478 was still owing.

WESLEYAN METHODISM IN PLYMOUTH.

OPENING OF KING-STREET SUNDAY-SCHOOLS.

Amongst the numerous religious bodies in Plymouth none is more keenly alive to the necessities of the times than the Wesleyan Methodists, and yesterday saw the completion of yet another of the numerous aggressive enterprises which this connexion has successfully undertaken. The occasion was the opening of the new Sunday-school premises attached to King-street Church. The sad calamity which marred the stone-laying ceremony in October last, though still fresh in the minds of many who were taking part in the proceedings yesterday, had the effect of stimulating the workers to greater activity in order to make up as far as possible for the monetary loss which that melancholy incident involved; and with bright weather and hopeful surroundings, the new building was opened under the most auspicious and encouraging circumstances.

With the additions recently made, the King-street Wesleyan body can now boast of the possession of one of the largest and most commodious connexional centres of religious activity to be found in the West, and one that is rivalled by few others in the country. The cost of the new schools is about £3,000. Built of local stone with buff-facing bricks, the added structure comprises a spacious lecture-hall capable of holding about 400 people, two classrooms for infants, large enough to accommodate 250 scholars; a young men's meeting-room, the size of which is equal to the two class-rooms combined, and other conveniences. The upper storey includes a large schoolroom, where 500 scholars can be seated; seven smaller classrooms, a library, a tea-room, and a ladies' lavatory and cloakroom. The entrance hall is a spacious one, and the pitchpine staircase broad and substantial in appearance. The woodwork throughout the premises is of pitchpine. Ample provision has been made for the admission of an abundance of light, and also for efficiently heating the rooms; and special attention has been devoted to the matter of ventilation, Boyle's patent foul air extractors having been brought into use.

Sunday School extension opened in early Summer, 1895.

Tragedy at Stone Laying

The Stone Laying ceremony for the extension of 1894 had just begun when a temporary platform collapsed injuring 41 spectators and killing one, Mrs. Mary Rowan.

The ceremony was abandoned and the twelve children who had been waiting to lay stones bearing the initials of the original Sunday School Teachers were hurried away. These stones can now be seen relaid from the original church, in the wall enclosing the garden of the present church.

Nine Hundred on Roll

It is reputed that in 1871 there had been 603 children on the roll. In 1880, 849, in 1890, 856, in 1900, 911, and in 1910, it reached a peak of 939 Sunday School scholars.

Cottage Prayer Meetings

The early teachers formed themselves into Bands of Prayer Leaders and held Cottage Prayer Meetings all over the district; ten to twelve meetings weekly at one time. In this way young local preachers were helped in their training until the opening of the Mission rooms and the birth of the Millbay Band.

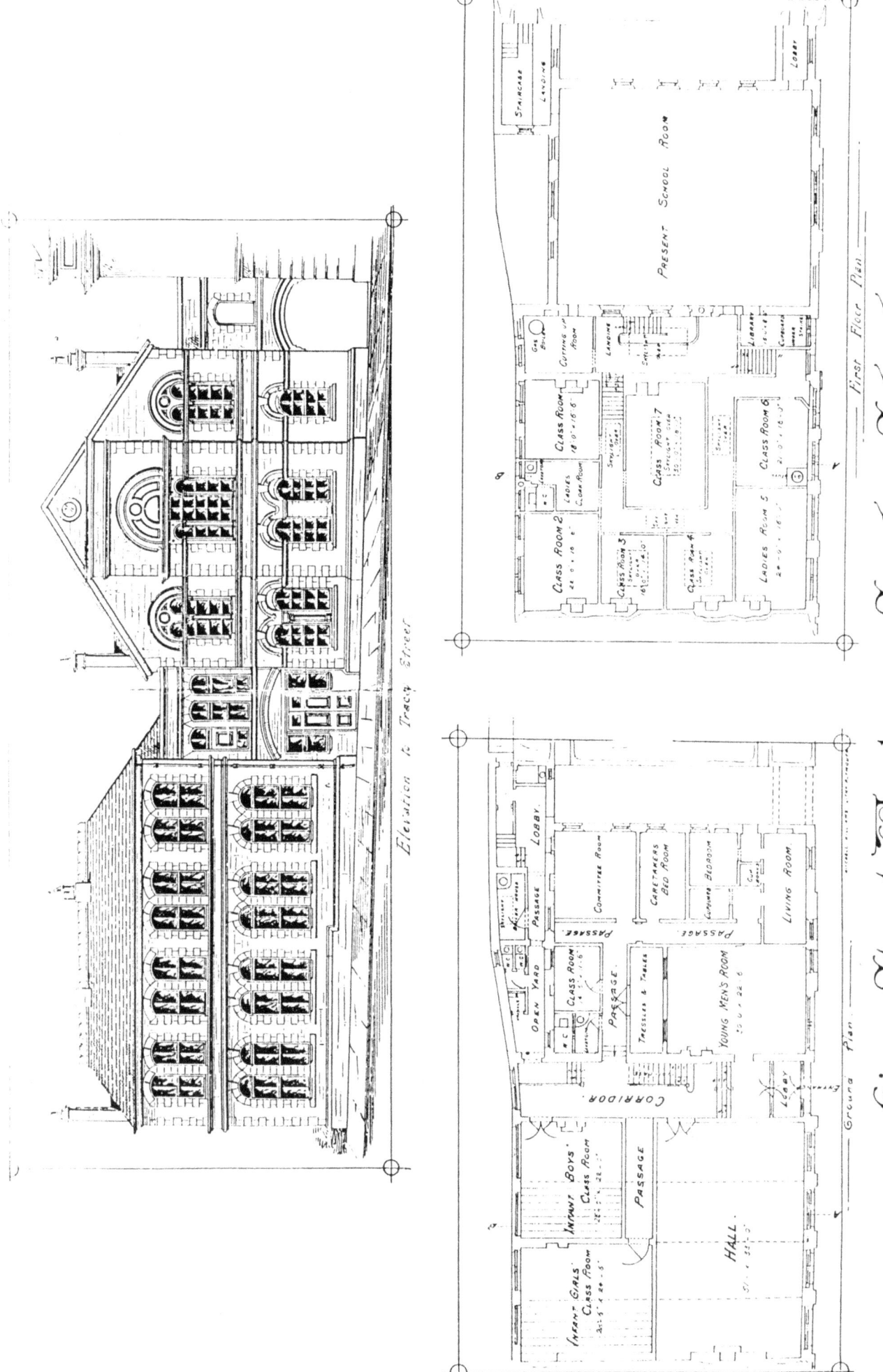

First to Modernize

Not long after the completion of the Sunday School extension the leaders and teachers graded the school into departments. This followed a visit by Mr. G. H. Archibald and Miss Huntley, the pioneers of the Graded Movement.

In Easter 1909, Mr. and Mrs. Osborn, Miss Stoneman and Miss S. Almond visited the Conference at Bourneville and returned to organize the work at King Street so that by June 1909 the Primary Department was in working order. The Cradle Roll was established at the same time with Miss Gladys Spear in charge, helped by Miss Doris Helmore and Miss Vera Strout. King Street was one of the first in the West Country to adopt such 'modern' organization which in turn led to their having frequent visitors for many years, conducted through the various departments by Mr. William Spear as General Secretary.

Out of the Primary Department grew the Junior Department for 7 to 9 year olds taken on by Miss Lillie Stoneman in January 1910 with Mr. Stanley Helmore as Assistant Superintendent. The Beginner's Department was started under the leadership of Miss Almond who supervised Miss Lily Hodgess.

ON SEVENTIETH BIRTHDAY

Plymouth Church Rededicated

WITH an inscribed silver key Miss Violet Winnicott yesterday reopened King-street Methodist Church, Plymouth, for public worship.

The church has been closed for four months for complete renovation, an undertaking rendered possible by a generous gift of £1,000 towards the cost by Sir Frederick Winnicott, a former Mayor of Plymouth, in memory of his brother, Ald. Richard Winnicott, who was closely connected with the Sunday-school and the church.

After Miss Winnicott had opened the door, the waiting congregation, which numbered many hundreds, filed into the main body of the church, and saw, many of them for the first time, the redecorated interior.

The teak grain of the woodwork contrasts richly with the lighter decorative scheme of the walls. Electric light installations and fittings are entirely new, and many minor repairs and improvements have been effected.

Following the reopening of the church, Rev. G. Leonard Robinson, chairman of the district, "solemnly and properly" rededicated it, exactly 70 years after the church was first opened for public worship.

20 Morgan Street,
St. Paul's,
Bristol. 2.
Feb 22. 1940

Dear Sir,

I trust you will excuse me writing to you, but I feel it is my duty to write and thank you for your kindness to the forces especially my son. He was called to the colours Jan. 17th and sent to Plymouth, not knowing the town or anyone he felt very lonesome untill he heard of your (Service mens rooms.) Since then he writes his letters and so enjoys his sunday tea with you. He continually writes and tells me what a blessing your rooms and all are to him. I also had a sailor visit me from the north sea who wanted to see my son, when I told him if he could not find him at the (Ballard Barracks.) he would find him at your mens rooms his reply was I know the place only to well its been a blessing to hundreds of us

Generous Gift Pays for Complete Renovation in 1936

Wednesday, March 4th, 1936, was the date for the re-opening of the church after the complete renovation had taken place. This had been made possible through a generous gift from Alderman Sir Frederick Winnicott, J.P., in memory of his brother, the late Alderman Richard Winnicott. Evening services had been held at the Guildhall whilst renovation took place, with morning services in the schoolroom.

The celebrations started with a Public Luncheon at 1.30 p.m., the re-opening ceremony was at 3.15 p.m., with the Reverend James Beckett presiding. Miss Violet Winnicott opened the doors and a sermon was given by Leslie F. Church. Miss Gwen Fugler sang 'Bless this House.'

Tickets for the tea which followed in the school hall cost 9 pence. Later there was an organ recital by Mr. H. Woodward and a Thanksgiving meeting. Just five years after the renovation the church was bombed.

October 20th, 1915.

Forces Canteen Twice Over

When war broke out in 1914 the school buildings were used as a Forces' Canteen. At that time Reverend Harold C. Morton was the Minister. A canteen, rest, writing and recreation room was opened throughout the week, while a Mrs. Tubb and her helpers provided Sunday afternoon teas for hundreds of servicemen. After the evening service they gathered for community singing, coffee and family prayers. 25 years later at the outbreak of the 2nd World War King Street saw a repeat procedure in 1939.

Sunday tea in the Second World War.

SUNDAY TEA AT SERVICE MENS ROOM, KING STREET METHODIST CHURCH, PLYMOUTH

Over 5,000 names in the Visitors' Book

Mrs. Stella Payne remembered pianists playing to entertain the troops, some 5,000 of whom signed the visitors' book, and the inhabitants coming into the church from the nearby streets after a bombing raid. She recalled sheltering in the corridor during choir practice the night before the church was destroyed.

Blitz Night — Friday, 21st March, 1941

Plymouth experienced the first raid of the war on Saturday, July 6th 1940, but it was in the intense raids of March 1941 that King Street was destroyed.

Thursday, March 20th, and Friday, March 21st, were two terrifying nights when Plymouth's shopping centre was wiped out, in almost identical 4 hour raids, the first taking place only two hours after the King and Queen had paid their first visit to Plymouth.

Sirens Go

Mr. Harry Deans recalled hearing the sirens somewhere around 7.30 p.m. on the Friday night, and looking out to see the main road glow with thousands of incendiaries that lit the way for the following heavy bombs. He said that it was between 9 — 9.30 p.m. that the bomb fell on King Street, falling into the courtyard which separated the Chapel Keeper's house from the church vestries and organ loft. The fire which followed gutted the entire church building; the Great Hall was left roofless and the Keeper's house was destroyed. The upstairs of the Sunday School buildings was gone but enough of the Sunday School buildings were left for church life to continue for the next fourteen years!

King Street became one of twenty thousand properties destroyed or damaged in those two nights; a rough estimate of cost being £100,000,000 worth of damage in the city.

> S. Tugwell
> 101 Mess. D. G. Camp
> Rifle Range
> Portland
> Apr. 4th
>
> Dear Sir,
>
> Many thanks for your kindly thoughts, and also the committee's, and Friends of King Street Church. I was pleased to receive your Christmas Gift & Card. This is late to answer I know, but I with others, are engaged on special work, and at all times, and anytime we are called on to perform work, which will and does protect our Merchant Ships from the enemy's Magnetic Mine. You may have heard Mr Winston Churchill, speak of the special work that our particular body of Men are carrying out, and I am pleased to be able to tell you, with great success. It is nice to know, that while we are away from our homes, you and your helpers, have us all in your thoughts, and the work that you are doing

Servicemen received letters and gifts from the church.

Incendiary bombs destroyed the old stone building on the night of March 21, 1941, despite the efforts of Boys' Brigade members who acted as fire-watchers.

The pews burned "like matchwood" and incendiaries which had lodged in the roof caused its collapse.

Worship continued without a break in the smaller of the Sunday school halls, which had been heavily damaged along with 20 classrooms that formed part of the church.

Worship as Usual

Saturday morning following the destruction, it was found that the Lecture Hall was still intact, so this was cleared in order to use it for Sunday Service. A sign was placed on the wall stating that it was to be, "Worship As Usual."

"Yes God Is Good"

Sunday morning, March 23rd, Reverend Hickling opened the morning service on the steps of the bombed church and then they continued in the Lecture Hall, Jack Adams choosing the hymn, "Yes God Is Good." As Mrs. Payne recalled — "It was quite hard to sing that morning." In future years on the anniversary of the bombing, services were opened on the church steps.

Found in the Rubble

Some weeks later the charred remains of the silver communion plate were found in the rubble and even, Mrs. Payne said — Mrs. Beckley's collection in an envelope!

```
                              K.J. Fowell, Writer,
                              R 8 Mess,
                                R.N. Barracks,
                                    DEVONPORT.

                         6th January 1940.



Dear Mr. Woodall,
          Thank you very much indeed for the parcel
which you kindly sent me. All the good things contained
in it were very acceptable and perhaps you will kindly
express to the Stewards, on my behalf, my thanks for their
contribution.

          In particular I welcomed the Prayer Book and
Testament. In these troublesome times I consider much
satisfaction and strength is gained from prayer and
consequently the books will be my constant companion and
comfort wherever I go.

          On the threshold of the New Year it is
impossible to forecast what the coming days have in store.
But I am always conscious of the great help and advice I
have received from your teachings and talks at the Chapel.
The satisfaction thus gained, and the very pleasant memories
of our past association, will, I am sure, assist me in great
measure, to face any difficulties that may lie before me.

          With best wishes for your good health and
happiness in the coming year,

                         Yours sincerely,

                              L. Fowell
```

Hall becomes Chapel

The remaining lecture hall was turned into a chapel with the use of appropriate furnishings and the memorial stained-glass window given by the youth in memory of youth club President Mr. W. Brimmell. The youth club also presented the church with the altar cross in memory of the service of the Reverend Fred Hickling. The lecture hall was used for church activities for 14 years after the bombing.

Mr. Gerald Payne remembered that on Wednesday evenings various sections of the church provided entertainment in order to raise funds for rebuilding. Tickets were not to cost more than 1 shilling.

The font and some other pieces made for the lecture hall by Mr. Harry Deans and Edgar Payne were later given to Brixton Methodist Church.

It should not be Rebuilt

Conference Commission's Report in 1947 felt that the church should not be rebuilt and war damage payment should be used at Crownhill.

In a Special Quarterly Meeting held at Mutley on Friday, 28th March, 1947, it was "Resolved that this meeting is in complete sympathy with the King Street Leaders and Trustees in their opposition to the suggestion that King Street should not be rebuilt..."

Plans to rebuild were formed.

2. REPLANNING PROBLEMS

(a) King Street.

However regrettable on the ground of historic association, it is clear to the Commission that the replanning of Plymouth and the dispersal of so large a proportion of the population previously resident in the centre of the City makes it obvious that King Street should not be rebuilt. In any case, the site of King Street will be required in the replanning proposals and the Commission feels that that part of the City will be adequately provided for by the Plymouth Central Hall. No adequate reason exists, as we say later, for putting a new King Street in the Stonehouse area. With a desire to make a definitely constructive proposal the Commission submits:

1. That due provision should be made for the continuance of the work of the Sunday Schools, women's meetings and the like now being carried on in the King Street premises.

2. That King Street by means of the portable war damage payment should be replaced on a suitable site in reach of the new housing areas. It submits that Crownhill offers a most suitable suggestion and that the importance of this centre will be evident.

"A Sad End..."

"It is a sad end for walls so true and strong, so well-built and enduring...." said the minister and chairman of the Plymouth Methodist Circuit Reverend Frederick A. Rowe at the evening thanksgiving service on Wednesday, January 4th, 1956 following the 4 p.m. closing service. Mr. Lawrence Bond Spear (hereafter to be referred to as Jack) presided with speakers Reverend Albert Fenn and Mr. Kenneth Cooke who spoke on the history of the church.

The following Sunday the Sunday School met for the last time in the old premises and on January 15th, marched, led by the Boys' Brigade to the Nissen hut chapel in Royal Parade.

CITY CHURCH CLOSES AFTER CENTURY

King-Street Methodists Will Build Again In The Crescent

PLYMOUTH'S King-street Methodist Church closes tonight after a century of worship, interrupted by severe bomb damage in the blitz. A new church is to be built soon in The Crescent.

At 4 p.m. there will be a service conducted by the Rev. Frederick A. Rowe, minister of the church and chairman of the Plymouth Methodist Circuit, and at 7 p.m. will be held a service of thanksgiving.

Mr. L. Bond Spear, secretary of the trust, will preside, and speakers will be the Rev. Albert H. Fenn and Mr. A. Kenneth Cook, circuit steward and chapel steward at King-street.

The move has been necessitated because the remains of the old building have to be removed to make way for new roads and buildings.

SHOP AS CHAPEL

Worship will be transferred to 5, George-street, a temporary shop which will be known as the chapel.

Sunday morning services will be held here and evening services at the Royal Assembly Hall in Lockyer-street, while Sunday school and other Sunday and week-day gatherings will meet in the chapel part of 1, George-street, and 7, Westwell-gardens, now to be known as Wesley Hall.

Next Sunday the Sunday school will meet for the last time in the old premises and on January 15 will assemble in King-street and march to the chapel, Royal-parade, led by The Boys' Brigade Band.

Number 5, George Street

Last service in the Lecture Hall, Wednesday, January 4th 1956.

KING STREET METHODIST
CHURCH, PLYMOUTH.

We have to announce that our Premises are to be Demolished to make way for new buildings. We shall build a New Church in The Crescent. Meanwhile our work will continue, as usual, in temporary accommodation.

We INVITE OLD SCHOLARS and all others associated with us through the years to ATTEND the FINAL SERVICES to be held on these premises

SUNDAY, JANUARY 1st, 1956.
11.0 a.m The Rev. ALBERT H. FENN.
3.0 p.m Annual Convenant Service.
6.30 p.m. The Rev. FREDERICK A. ROWE, M.A Anthem: "Hallelujah Chorus." (Beethoven) After this Service a Social Hour, when the Plymouth Ladies' Choir will give a Programme of Music. Thankoffering for the new church.

WEDNESDAY, JANUARY 4th.
CLOSING SERVICES AT KING STREET.
4.0 p.m Divine Worship conducted by the Rev. FREDERICK A. ROWE, M.A., Minister of the Church and chairman of the Plymouth Methodist District.
5.15 p.m PUBLIC TEA. Price 1/- each.
7.0 p.m Service of Thanksgiving for King Street 1866-1956, and of Dedication to the King Street 1956 onwards: Chairman: Mr. L. BOND SPEAR, B.A Speakers: The Rev. ALBERT H. FENN, Mr. A KENNETH COOKE, B.Sc. Anthems by the Choir: "Gloria" (Mozart) "Praise the Lord" (Elvey), "Hallelujah Chorus" (Handel) Choirmaster: Mr. B. R. HARPER. B.Sc.

Lecture Hall:- last Harvest, 1955.

REBUILDING OF CHURCH MAY BE NEARER

POSSIBLE EFFECT OF COUNCIL MOVE

BECAUSE Plymouth City Corporation is applying for a compulsory purchase order for 3.05 acres of land in The Crescent for further development schemes, the rebuilding of King-street Methodist Church may have been brought nearer.

King-street Methodist Church, which was opened in 1866, was entirely destroyed in the early days of the last war, and for the past 14 years the work of the church has been carried on in the Sunday school.

At a public inquiry in 1947 the Corporation was granted a compulsory order for part of the site and the land on which the Sunday school now stands. At the same time it gave the church trustees a verbal undertaking that it would grant a similar equivalent site on which to rebuild the church in the central area.

PLANS APPROVED

In March, 1948, a site bounded by The Crescent and Gooseberry-hill and facing the Continental Hotel was set aside for Church purposes. Architects were instructed to prepare plans, and in August last year drawings of the new church were submitted to the Corporation for approval. This was received last month.

Meanwhile the church trustees have been informed that they must be prepared to quit the King-street premises by January, 1956, to enable the building of Cornwall-street to proceed. The question of alternative accommodation has therefore to be considered.

The Corporation has intimated it is prepared to allow the use of the Royal Assembly Rooms for Sunday services.

This is a matter about which the trustees are not altogether happy. They feel that if they could be granted a licence and allowed to proceed with rebuilding without restriction they would be able to complete the church in the year that must elapse before the move has to be made.

March 1955. Plans approved.

The Trustees are to receive £5,000 from American Methodists, who gave £30,000 to restore historic Methodist churches which suffered in the war.

They are also being helped by war-damage compensation, compensation from Plymouth Corporation for the acquisition of their old site for the proposed Pannier Market, and by efforts over the past 14 years of members who have kept up their loyalty to the Church.

A LETTER FROM THE MINISTER

Dear Friend,

I am writing to tell you about the closing down of our work in Tracey Street and the plans for its transfer to the City Centre.

Our beloved Church was destroyed in 1941, but the premises that remained have been the scene of intensive endeavour in the years that have followed. Now they must come down, to make way for the new roads and buildings in the western part of Plymouth. It is our intention to build a lovely Church, with adequate accommodation for all our work, not far away, at the western end of The Crescent, in the heart of the City. This great enterprise will begin soon.

Meanwhile we must move to other quarters, and our work will be housed as follows:—

Sunday Morning Worship 11 a.m. *at No. 5 George Street in Royal Parade, the shop which is directly opposite the Scotch Wool and Hosiery Stores in Royal Parade. Our name remains the same, and you will see "King Street Methodist Church" over the windows. This shop will be known as The Chapel, and will be suitably furnished.*

Sunday Evening Worship at 6.30 p.m. *at the Royal Assembly Hall, Lockyer Street (entrance Athenaeum Place), where there is comfortable accommodation for a large congregation—will you help to make it large?*

Our Sunday School and other Sunday and weekday gatherings *will meet in (1) The Chapel. (2) part of No. 1 George Street (the shop called Louise Hats) to be known as The Sunday School. (3) No. 7 Westwell Gardens, formerly a shop, now to be known as Wesley Hall.*

All our activities will continue, and with good will and patience we shall soon settle down to the new conditions and find fresh opportunities of service at the centre of the City.

You will find set out in this leaflet our arrangements for the closing Services at Tracey Street and the first Services in the new premises. King Street has been a centre of vital Christian work for nearly a century, and we shall meet to honour Him Who has blessed so signally the labours of His people here, and to dedicate ourselves to the new venture now beginning. I am sure I do not appeal in vain, in this hour of change and opportunity, for a worthy response from all who love 'King Street, Plymouth'.

Yours sincerely,

FREDERICK A. ROWE.

Harvest in the Nissen Hut, 1956.

OPENING OF TEMPORARY METHODIST CHURCH

Dedication service in Plymouth

Sunday, January 8th, 1956.

FROM eleven o'clock yesterday morning, No. 5, George-street, Plymouth, held a special significance for hundreds of Plymouth Methodists. It was then that the first service in the new premises of the King-street Methodist Church was held before a large congregation.

The chapel was dedicated by the minister, the Rev. Frederick A. Rowe.

Before the service, each member of the church was welcomed to the new premises by Deaconess Sister Nora Trineman.

As the clock of St. Andrew's Church struck the hour, the minister, accompanied by the secretary of the trust, Mr L. B. Spear, the society steward, Mr. E. Payne, and the chapel steward, Mr A. K. Cooke, arrived at the main door to stand outside while the congregation sang a hymn.

Door unlocked

Then Mr. Rowe knocked on the doors. He was welcomed by Mr. Adams on behalf of the trustees, leaders and members of the King-street Church.

The door was then unlocked by Mrs Rowe, the wife of the minister, and the keys presented to him.

Following the ceremony of dedication, a procession consisting of the minister, Sister Trineman, Mrs. Rowe, and Messrs. L. B. Spear, A. E. Cooke, and J. Adams, moved into the body of the chapel for the ordinary morning service.

The new premises, which will be the temporary home of King-street Methodists, were formerly shops.

During the week a band of volunteers, in the charge of Mr. Adams transformed the building into a chapel which will hold a congregation of 230.

Fittings

Many of the fittings were transferred from the old King-street Church, including Communion plate, damaged during the blitz in 1941, and a memorial stained glass window, made for the refurnishing of the old building after the war.

Alternative accommodation is also situated in Westwell-gardens.

The old King-street church was badly damaged in the air raids of 1941 and is now due for total demolition to make way for new roads and buildings.

A new church is to be built in the Crescent, and, it is expected, will be ready in about two years' time.

Last service

In the afternoon the last Sunday school service to be held at King-street—coupled with the annual promotion service—was held at the old church. Some 120 children attended.

The service was taken by Mr. E. Payne, general superintendent of the Sunday school, with Sister Trineman deputising for the minister.

Mr. T. Batten and Mr. Lawrence Spear spoke to the children.

King Street Methodist Church, Plymouth

WILL YOU HELP US TO CHANGE THIS . . . .

INTO THIS . . . .

. . . . by joining with us in WORSHIP and SERVICE, NOW, so that "King Street, Plymouth," may soon be established in The Crescent.

WE CORDIALLY INVITE YOU TO HELP US IN THIS GREAT ENTERPRISE

Breaking the Ground Ceremony

On Saturday, February 11th, 1956, 150 people attended the "Breaking of the Ground ceremony" for the building of new King Street.

The day was bitterly cold and Mrs. Spear remembered that the ground was so hard that it had to be heated by braziers before the ceremony so that the turves could be cut. (Mr. Jack Spear also remembered that the new spades used to cut these turves were sold to add to the building funds).

The ceremony began when the minister said, "Let the ground be broken and let the work of the building of this church to the glory of God proceed."

Seven Diggers

There were seven representatives of the church chosen to break the ground: the Superintendent minister, Reverend A. H. Fenn, Reverend F. Rowe the minister, Mr. J. Adams, Mr. A. K. Cooke chapel stewards, Mr. Jack Spear, secretary of the Trust, Mr. T. H. Deans and Miss Joan Wallis the Sunday School Queen, representing the Sunday School.

The building of the new church, estimated at £156,000 was to begin.

Sun for the Stone Laying

On the morning of Wednesday, July 18th, 1956, it poured! At midday however, the weather changed suddenly to give a lovely sunny afternoon and evening.

The first service of the afternoon was held at the temporary chapel, led by the Reverend F. Hickling, the 400 people attending overflowing into the car park.

KING STREET METHODIST CHURCH, PLYMOUTH

The Superintendent Minister of the Circuit,
the Minister of the Church and the Trustees invite

The Senior Chapel Steward and Mrs. Adams

to the

Stonelaying Ceremony

on WEDNESDAY, 18th JULY, 1956, at 6.30 p.m.

on THE NEW SITE, in MILLBAY ROAD, PLYMOUTH

The Foundation Stone will be laid on behalf of the Trustees by
MR. H. LAWRENCE SPEAR

R.S.V.P.—L. B. SPEAR,
132 Eggbuckland Road,
Plymouth.   P.T.O.

Mr. H. L. Spear receives a silver trowel and then a mallet.

Then followed the actual stone-laying ceremony at the church site conducted by the Superintendent of the circuit, Reverend Fenn, with three lessons read by Reverend E. Bower of Pomphlett.

An estimated 1,500 people were there to witness the stone-laying with the congregation including the Lord and Lady Mayoress of Plymouth — Mr. and Mrs. W. J. Oats, and Lady Nancy Astor. There were also 4 women present who had laid stones back in 1894 when the Tracey Street extension was founded. They were Mrs. Olive Mitchelmore, Mrs. Nellie Gould, Mrs. Lydia Sweet and Miss Violet Winnicott.

The Stone is Laid

Mr. Jack Adams placed a glass jar in the cavity beneath the stone itself. This jar had been rescued from beneath the foundation stone at Tracey Street.

Representing the trustees, Mr. H. Lawrence Spear then laid the foundation stone, with a trowel presented on behalf of the architects by Mr. William Marsden. Prayers led by the minister Reverend Rowe then followed.

Later gifts were placed on the foundation stone itself and dedicated by Reverend John H. Chamberlayne of Peverell. The Salvation Army Band accompanied the singing. A further meeting of prayer and praise took place in the temporary chapel with an estimated 600 present.

What was in the Glass Jar?

The jar originally contained:
1. Three coins of 1893, valued at one penny, sixpence and one shilling.
2. A list of Trustees — 21 in number.
3. A programme of the placing of the memorial stones of the new Sunday School building on Wednesday, 3rd October, 1894. (Luncheon for the day costing 2 shillings and sixpence).
4. A leaflet about the new extension.
5. A circuit plan for part of 1894.
6. A copy of the Western Daily Mercury and Western Morning News where a complete ladies' outfit was advertised for £1.8.6d.
7. A copy of the Methodist Recorder at 1 penny each for 27th September, 1894.

These original contents were removed to be safely kept and the jar was then refilled with the following items.
1. A small copy of the Bible.
2. A circuit plan for April—June, and July—September, 1956.
3. The Methodist Recorder for July 5th, 1956 (Conference).
4. The Western Morning News and The Western Evening Herald of 18th July.
5. A specimen of Stone-laying Ceremony note paper.
6. The agenda of the June Quarterly Meeting of the Circuit, 7th June, 1956.

Mr. Jack Spear told me that the next day he was able to go down to the site and retrieve the jar in order that he could put in a newspaper account of the previous day's ceremony.

Work in progress.

Topping Out Ceremonies
On July 26th, 1957, the topmost brick was laid on the Northern Gable of the church by Miss Lily Goad, one of the few lady trustees.

On the 16th August, 1957, the topmost brick was laid on the Southern Gable by Miss Muriel Goad.

The northern gable above the main entrance.

The tufret, or fleche, on the church roof has been removed from the final plans as "something that can go in cold storage" in order to effect an economy.

Bricks for the Youth Hall

About a year after the Stonelaying a Bricklaying Ceremony for the present Youth Hall took place on the 20th July, 1957. It was a wet, cold and windy Saturday.

Reverend Grose conducted a short service before the actual ceremony. On the platform with him were Mr. Jack Spear, Trust Secretary, Sister Nora Trineman, deaconess, Mr. J. Adams, chapel and Society Steward, and Mr. E. Payne, Sunday School Superintendent.

Reverend Grose laid the first of an estimated 200 bricks placed that evening. He was followed by Sister Nora and the platform party, the Sunday School Queen Miss Wendy Partridge, and members of the Sunday School and church departments. A large number of very young children with their mothers also laid bricks.

Sister Nora Trineman and Rev. R. E. Grose.

First bricks of Methodist youth hall laid

NEARLY 100 people stood in the rain and cold wind on Saturday to watch the first bricks laid of the Youth Hall of the Methodist Church being built at The Crescent, Millbay-road, Plymouth.

The bricks were laid by officers and members of the Sunday School.

Before the actual bricklaying ceremony, a brief service was conducted by the Rev. R. E. Grose, and with him on the platform were the secretary of the Trust (Mr. L. Bond Spear), Sister Nora Trineman, Mr. J. Adams (chapel and society steward), and Mr. E. Payne (Sunday School superintendent).

It was estimated that more than 200 bricks were laid during the evening, and the ceremony started with Mr. Grose laying the first of them. Then followed Sister Trineman, Mr. Adams, Mr. Spear, Mr. Payne, and the Sunday School Queen, 14-year-old Miss Wendy Partridge.

QUEUE FORMED

After her came two other former queens, the Misses Wendy Phillips and Joan Wallis, and a queue formed, consisting of the leaders of the church's various departments, and children from the Primary, Junior, and Senior Sunday Schools, and members of the Bible Class.

A large number of very young children, with their mothers, also laid bricks.

The new church, which is replacing the blitzed King-street Methodist Church, and is to bear its name, is well on the way to completion, and is expected to open for worship at the end of the year.

Halfpennies help

Edgar Payne issued cards to the Sunday School so that they could collect ship-halfpennies to help towards the fund-raising for the construction.

The New King Street Church is Opened without a Key. December 4th, 1957

The day's ceremonies started with a dinner at the Duke Of Cornwall Hotel. During the after dinner speech, Sir Percy Thomas the architect of King Street revealed that, "There's no lock on the door so all Miss Almond has to do is to push it." However Miss Mabel Almond, the opener of the New King Street, whose family had been connected with the church from the earliest days, was presented with a gilt key which would have opened the lock had it been fixed in time!

Silver Salver

During the celebratory dinner, Mr. Jack Spear was presented with an inscribed silver salver for his work as prime mover in the rebuilding. This was etched with a picture of the church.

The Bishop of Plymouth, Dr. Norman Clarke wished the new church, 'God Speed' and expressed his congratulations on the venture. He hoped to see a real unity between the recently reconstructed St.Andrew's Parish Church and King Street.

Civic congratulations were extended by the Lord Mayor, Leslie Paul.

A toast was made to the architects, Percy Thomas and Sons, Cardiff, and to the contractors, John Garrett and Sons, and quantity surveyors, Langdon and Every.

Fog Delays Opening

Dr. Harold Roberts, President of the Methodist Conference for that year, had been invited to dedicate the new church, but the Cornish Riviera Express bringing him from London was delayed by fog, causing the proceedings to be held up for half an hour. The Western Morning News, December 5th, 1957, reports that a fast car with a trustee, Mr. H. Lawry, waited at the station to rush him to the church.

Closed Circuit T.V.

Things finally got under way for the 550 people attending the service, whilst nearly as many watched on closed-circuit television in adjoining rooms.

Gathering of the Clergy

Many of the clergy were present, both Anglican and Free Church, including a former Superintendent minister, The Reverend Edgar Hines and three former ministers of the church — the Reverend Frederick Hickling, Reverend Frank Crump, and the Reverend Frederick A. Rowe.

The choir led the President of the Conference and the officiating and visiting ministers and church officers to the main door of the church where the Door Opening Ceremony took place.

The processional hymn was, "Praise My Soul The King Of Heaven" and the choir sang the anthem, "Behold the Tabernacle of God" by Dr. William H. Harris.

Lessons were read by Sister Nora Trineman, and Reverend David Ball secretary of the Plymouth and Exeter district.

Dedication

The dedication of the church by Dr. Roberts was followed by the dedication of the font, pulpit, and Communion table by the Reverend James Whitehead, chairman of the Plymouth and Exeter district, Reverend Lever and Reverend Grose respectively.

ORDER OF SERVICE

The Congregation being assembled in the Church, the doors shall be closed two minutes before the hour at which the Service is due to begin

The Congregation is invited to use the time of waiting before the commencement of the Dedication Service, in Silent Prayer both for those who will Minister and those who will Worship in this Church.

THE PRESIDENT OF THE CONFERENCE, together with Officiating and Visiting Ministers, and the Church Officers, all being preceded by the Choir, shall walk in Procession to the Main Door of the Church.

Knocking at the Door, the President shall say;

Open unto me the Gates of Righteousness ;
I will go into them and I will praise the Lord.

Within the Church, the Congregation standing upon the Knocking at the Door, the Senior Chapel Steward, Mr. J. S. Adams, together with the Junior Chapel Steward, Mr. T. H. Deans, shall approach the Opener, Miss M. L. Almond, and the Senior Steward shall say :

Madam, on behalf of the Minister, Trustees and Leaders of the King Street Methodist Church, I invite you to open the Door of our New Church, that it may be Dedicated to the Worship of Almighty God.

Whereupon the Chapel Stewards shall conduct the Opener to the Main Door of the Church which she shall open and shall say :

To the Glory of God, I declare this Church open.

Turning to the President of the Conference she shall say :

Sir, in token that this building has been erected for the Methodist Church, I deliver to you the key thereof, and pray you now to Dedicate it to the Worship of Almighty God.

The President of the Conference shall say :

In the name of the Methodist Church we accept the key, in token of the trust committed to us.

On passing through the Vestibule and on to the Threshold of the Church proper, the President shall pause and say :

Peace be to this Church, and all who worship therein.
Peace be to those that enter and to those that go out therefrom.
Peace be to those that love it, and that love the name of the Lord Jesus Christ.

THE PROCESSIONAL HYMN

Whilst this hymn is being sung, the Choir shall go to their places followed by the Minister of the Church, the Church Officers, the Opener, the Chapel Stewards, the Officiating and Visiting Ministers, The Superintendent Minister of the Circuit, The Chairman of the District, and The President.

Tea at the Central Hall

The opening service was followed by tea. The women of Central Hall, Mutley, Peverell Park, and Compton Methodist churches arranged a tea in the Central Hall, Saltash Street, for the price of 1 shilling and 6 pence each.

Just Finished

Mr. Harry Deans told me that the pulpit had been finished only just in time for the great day with last minute plans. Another cause for concern was whether the completed pulpit was actually going to get through the door to be erected in place. Luckily it did, with a few centimetres to spare.

Similarly in 1959, Mary Bolt was able to finish the embroidered pulpit fall after hundreds of hours of work, just in time for the Deaconess Convocation.

Thanksgiving Service

The church was again full in the evening for a Thanksgiving service. The choir sang two anthems that night — "Whoso dwelleth under the defence of the Most High" by G. C. Martin and, "Hallelujah" by Handel.

The Trust Treasurer, Mr. E. de Jersey Robin told this gathering that the site had cost £8,200 and on completion would be about £125,000. "Our own members, numbering only 240 or 250 have contributed over £7,000 since 1941 by many various efforts," he said.

A further £800 was raised on this day.

Some deep wells had had to be filled in with concrete as the site had at one time been that of an old hotel. This, and the hope which did not materialise that the City Council would grant a flatter site, had added to delays and expense.

"This is the End"

Reverend J. K. Whitehead paid tribute to the faith and perseverance of the members of the church:

"There must have been some who said: 'This is the end' in 1941. Rebuilding must have seemed an impossibility. But today the impossibility has been achieved."

Mr. Spear, chairing the service said that the moment was one of the proudest in the lives of the congregation.

"God and Drabness are Sworn Enemies"

Mr. Harper told me that Mr. Jack Spear suggested that the 48 strong choir should be robed. Consequently they became the first choir in the Plymouth and Exeter district to wear robes with the first occasion being the dedication day, Wednesday, December 4th.

Reverend Edward Lewis, President of Free Churches said of the choir that day, "The choirs' costume is simple and dignified while sufficiently assertive to suggest that God and drabness are sworn enemies."

Asbury House declared Open
Saturday, June 28th, 1958, at 6.30 p.m.

Methodist school 'link with American brothers'

THE Rev. Dr. E. Benson Perkins, a past president of the Methodist Conference and secretary of the World Methodist Council, on Saturday opened and dedicated Asbury House, the Sunday school extension of King-street Methodist Church.

Emphasising that the opening of the extension would strengthen links with American Methodists, Dr. Benson Perkins said that it was largely by their help that it had been built.

By the direction of the Connexional Chapel Committee, a gift of £5,000 had been made to the church from Methodists in America.

He recalled that in 1771 John Wesley sent Francis Asbury to found Methodism in America, and to become the first Methodist bishop in that country.

"By naming the Sunday school extension Asbury House rather than Church House, we thus recognise our links with our brothers from the other side of the Atlantic, and this will be a perpetual reminder to us all."

He added that Asbury House, which adjoins Wesley Hall, would provide at first-floor level small residential flats for the deaconess, Sister Nora Trineman, and for a permanent caretaker.

At ground level there were four rooms to accommodate the beginners' and primary departments of the Sunday school, a creche for the Sisterhood, rooms for Fellowship Class meetings, and an office for the Sunday school. It was hoped that a room might be furnished and equipped as a parlour or retiring-room for the women of the church and congregation.

A short service opened the ceremony, conducted by the Rev. Clifford Lever, superintendent minister of the Plymouth King-street Circuit, assisted by the Rev. Sydney Quick, minister of Peverell Park Methodist Church, and the Rev. R. E. Grose, minister of the church.

After the ministers and congregation had entered the building Miss Hilda L. Mitchell officially opened the class meeting-room. Mrs. J. Norman the general church room, Miss Marlene Cooper, the Sunday School Queen, the creche and nursery, and Miss Elizabeth E. Stoneman the Sunday school.

A closing service was held in Wesley Hall, followed by light refreshments.

Who was he?

Francis Asbury (1745-1816) was the founder of American Methodism. He was born in Birmingham. It seemed appropriate that Reverend Dr. E. Benson Perkins should come from Birmingham to open Asbury House as he was a past President of the Methodist Conference and the British secretary of the World Methodist Council, which helped to emphasize the links with American Methodism.

Gift of £5,000 from the Americans

Early in the war Methodists in America raised a substantial amount of money for rebuilding churches which were war damaged. King Street received through the connexional Chapel Committee, a gift of £5,000. In gratitude for this gift what might have otherwise been known as 'Church House' was to be known as 'Asbury House'.

Reverend Perkins declared Asbury House open after speaking briefly with the words, "In the Faith of Our Lord Jesus Christ, I dedicate the Building to the Glory of God; In The Name of the Father, and of the Son and of the Holy Ghost. Amen."

The Officiating Ministers, with others, shall then enter ASBURY HOUSE and shall pause in the corridor, whilst each of the Four Class Rooms shall be declared open in turn, with the following words:

THE CLASS MEETING ROOM
To be opened by **MISS HILDA L. MITCHELL**, saying:
To the Glory of God
I declare this Room open for Work amongst the Society Classes of the King Street Methodist Church.

THE GENERAL CHURCH ROOM.
To be opened by **MRS. J. NORMAN**, saying:
To the Glory of God
I declare this Room open for the General use of the Members and Friends of the King Street Methodist Church.

THE CRECHE AND NURSERY.
To be opened by **MISS MARLENE COOPER**—*The Sunday School "Queen"*, saying:
To the Glory of God
I declare this Room open for Work amongst Nursery and Little Children.

THE SUNDAY SCHOOL ROOM.
To be opened by **MISS ELIZABETH E. STONEMAN**, saying:
To the Glory of God
I declare this Room open for Work amongst Boys and Girls.

THE CONGREGATION shall then follow into ASBURY HOUSE and go through it to WESLEY HALL where, in due time, when all shall be seated, the Superintendent Minister shall conduct a short service.

Mr. Spear recalled that the first proposed site was in King-street, but farther west than the original one. This was considered unsuitable and the Corporation suggested the site that was finally chosen.

"A condition of our having it was that we should rebuild on a portion of the site a house conforming with the Georgian architecture of The Crescent," Mr. Spear continued. "Therefore, we propose to erect a church house there, with four rooms for Sunday school and society classes, which may also be used for district purposes."

Conforming to the style of The Crescent.

It was intended that the two first floor flats were to be for a Deaconess and a Caretaker, and that the ground level rooms were to accommodate the Beginner's and Primary Departments of the Sunday School, a Creche for the Sisterhood, rooms for Fellowship and Class meetings and an office for the Sunday School and for other purposes.

One Room for a Rest

The opening programme adds: "One room may well be furnished for the ladies of our Church and congregation upon whose help on social occasions and at the traditionally Methodist 'tea meeting' we depend so heavily."

Asbury House stands on what was formerly known as Nos 11, 12, 13, The Crescent.

Dedication of the New Organ

On Wednesday, 8th July, 1959, an invitation when all were welcome, was given for the Dedication, and Opening and Recital on the new organ.

Mr. Harry Stephens who had been a choir member for fifty years was invited from Holsworthy, to accept the organ from Mr. Stanley Lambert who represented Messrs. Nicholson and Co (Worcester) Ltd, who had constructed the organ. Mr. Stephens was to accept the key on behalf of the church and formally unlock the Organ Console, and then hand the key to Mr. Bertram Harper.

Reverend A. R. Martin the minister dedicated the organ.

After the service a Public Tea was held in Wesley Hall at the cost of 1 shilling and 6 pence per person.

Out of Tune

On this occasion Mr. Harper told me that he had a vivid recollection of every note on the electronic organ, which they had been using until the new organ was ready, being out of tune when he played it for the first part of the dedication service.

HISTORICAL NOTES

The Original Organ was built by Messrs. Conacher in 1869 for £400; it served us well being maintained and serviced by Messrs. Hele & Co., until in March 1941, it was destroyed when the Church itself fell a victim to enemy action.

Until 1903 the Choir, which has always played a prominent and helpful part in our Church life, owed dual allegiance—to an Organist, as well as to a Choirmaster. Through the years, there have been:—

Organists

1870—Mr. Fry, (assisted by an Organ blower)	1895—Mr. A. E. Hiorns
1870—Mr. Kent	1903—Mr. Harry Woodward
1870—Mr. Pearce	1944—Mr. Percy Chown
1878—Mr. Thomas Gaud	1948—Mr. B. R. Harper, B.Sc.

Choirmasters

1878—Mr. Edwin Roseveare	1895—Mr. J. Rule Palk

In 1878 no less than 11 organists applied for the vacant post, including, greatly daring, two ladies, the intrepid Miss Fanny Austin and Miss Ellen Atkins (who was blind). They were to get short shrift, however, for without more ado it was proposed, seconded and carried unanimously by the all-male Trust of that time, that "the ladies' names be cancelled". This left the field clear for Mr. Gaud to be appointed and he held the post for seventeen eventful years.

AFTER 37 years as organist at King Street Methodist Church, Bert Harper is set to retire as the church's regular organist on reaching his 80th birthday next month.

For some 25 years Mr Harper has been responsible for the production of a performance of Handel's Messiah, with an augmented choir, and the work has become a popular feature, drawing wide support locally.

His last production was Maunder's Olivet to Calvary, sung by the church choir, supported by the recently-formed Music Workshop, during last Sunday's evening service.

March, 1986.

Harry Woodward affectionately known as 'Daddy' Woodward remained organist for forty years. He was then followed by Mr. Percy Chown who kept the choir going during the post-war years until Mr. Bertram Harper took over.

To mark his retirement a party was held on April 17th, 1986 when well over 100 people sat down for a cooked meal provided by many church members and completed with a special iced cake made in the shape of a music book. A colour television set and flowers were presented to Mr. and Mrs. Harper.

Grand Opening Recital at 7.15 p.m.
The former minister of King Street, Reverend Grose, a musician himself had backed up plans for a three manual organ. He knew Professor Willis Grant, Professor of Music at Bristol University, and asked him to draw up the specifications for the new organ. He designed the organ to meet all requirements for the performance of organ music apart from the primary purpose of accompanying the services of the church. Professor Grant was invited to give the organ recital at 7.15 p.m.

SOME OTHER SPECIAL EVENTS

1895 King Street was chosen as the Conference Chapel.
1913 King Street again chosen for Conference, which this time marked the Missionary Centenary.
1929 King Street was used for conference at a time, the Handbook describes, when "There is a lessened interest generally in organised religion and church and parental interest and authority have declined."
1939 The Convocation of Deaconesses was based at King Street.
1959 The Convocation for this year was held from April 15—21st, 1959.
1965 King Street was used for many public meetings and the Sunday morning Conference Service
1966 Centenary Celebrations.

Let Your Light Shine
On Sunday, 16th November, 1969, after these and other chosen words spoken by Reverend David Hadfield on the entrance steps of the church, a frontal cross was illuminated, by Miss Elizabeth Stoneman.
In her will, Miss Margaret James who had been in Lillie Stoneman's fellowship group, asked that "an appropriate memorial" be placed in the church to a "very wonderful leader, Miss Lillie Stoneman."
This illuminated cross, now on automatic timer, shines out each evening over Western Approach.
Mrs. Mollie Hadfield told me that both she and her husband had felt that King Street was the happiest church and circuit they had worked in.

Stepping Stones — A Festival of Flowers.
8th—11th June, 1978

The 21st Anniversary of the re-building of the church was marked from the 8th—11th June by a Festival of Flowers.

"A very important Church"

At the opening of the Festival, 3 p.m. on 8th June, the Lord Mayor, Councillor W. E. Evans said that he was lucky enough to remember the original King Street before the Blitz. He described it as "A very important church which had played a vital part in the lives of many Plymouth people."

The Countess of Mount Edgecumbe who opened the Festival congratulated all those who had done the decorations. Guest of honour was the chairman of the Plymouth and Exeter District, the Reverend Amos Cresswell, who brought greetings from all the Methodists in his area.

The guests were presented with gifts of flowers by the oldest members of the church.

Stages of Life

The theme of the Festival decorations was 'Stepping Stones', with an arrangement from groups within the church covering the stages of life from baptism to marriage. The Festival included an art exhibition, organ recital, a concert by the Plymstock and District Choral Society and thanksgiving services on Sunday.

23rd September 1979 — Industrial Harvest Festival

Commemorative Window

Money was left by a Miss E. Warren to be enjoyed by her brothers. On their death in the early eighties an amount was left to the church on the condition that a coloured glass window was installed. Two designs were put forward and a vote was taken. The winning design was placed in the round window above the altar.

Many other church furnishings have been donated in memory of loved ones, including flower patterned altar kneelers worked in needlepoint by church members in memory of Mr. Edgar Payne.

1983 Plymouth was used again as a Conference City

* * *

This old sanctuary is a scene of very great animation as the hour of four o'clock draws near. Aisles are full of delegates, some arriving, others greeting, all expectant and apparently brimming over with high spirits. They murmur like children, like bees in summer in a hot garden. . . .

The place allotted to " the Press " is like a very deep front-line trench. We cannot see the occupants of the platform until they stand. Suddenly, over the parapet, we catch sight of Dr. Lightley, who has still to close his Presidential year. His head seems to spring out of a bowl of lovely roses adorning the desk of office. With a touch of the bell he resolves disorder and buzzing crowdiness into an assembly. We are " Conference " once again. Quickly we realise something of unity as we follow time-honoured and blessed custom in singing " All praise to our redeeming Lord," to the tune Abridge. The hymn was—in Dr. Dinsdale T. Young's words (used in his prayer)—our " united new song," and for each " a personal psalm."

* * *

Conference 1929.

Miss Sarah Almond and Miss Lizzie Stoneman cutting the Centenary cake in 1966.

SOME OF THE THINGS THEY DID THEN

Temperance work of the Band of Hope

With Mr. W. S. Spear as first Superintendent, the Band of Hope was formed in 1874 — one of its early activities being to deal with temperance work. It was described in the Sunday School Jubilee booklet as "An exceedingly useful institution for the propogation of total abstinence principles amongst scholars." Quite when the department ceased its educational work is not clear but it was certainly thriving in the first decades of the 20th century.

"Towards a true Christian Manliness"

The Boys' Brigade was formed in 1886 under the leadership of their Captain Mr. W. R. Hill. It was disbanded after two years but reformed in 1914 as the 10th Plymouth Company; its object being the advancement of habits of reverence, discipline, self respect, and all that tend towards a true Christian manliness."

The 1914 company had a band, and a weekly Bible class with a definite course of study, an ambulance class and a military drill practice which opened with singing from the Boys' Brigade Hymnal.

Sister Nora described the work of Captain and Mrs. Pester as outstanding while she was working at King Street in the post-war days; providing the boys with clothes and taking them to camp. Mr. Jack Spear was very much involved in the work, and in the late fifties, Mrs. Ella Cooke and Mrs. Joan Bolt. The Boys' Brigade continued until the early sixties.

Wesley Guild.

On October 16th the first Literary Evening of the Session was held, when Mrs. M. Burge was the speaker. Her subject was "Running and Reading," and showed how best we may enjoy reading in these busy days of ours. Miss K. B. Stuart was in the Chair.

In connection with the Christian Service Section of our Guild, we were grateful to Mrs. Walter Phere, of Cobourg Street, for a helpful address on "The Tower of Babel." Mr. V. Abraham was the Chairman for the evening.

Autumn 1933.

The Band of Hope

children gave an entertainment on Thursday, January 13th, when Mr. S. D. Venning presided. Rev. A. Barritt gave us an address, and Mrs. Barritt presented the monitors with medals. Four girls, trained under Sergeant Avery, gave a very splendid Indian club drill, and were encored. Mr. Harold Lear greatly interested us by his recitations. The programme which was miscellaneous was contributed to in the main by our own members. A collection to defray expenses was made with satisfactory results.

Winter 1910.

Mutual Improvement

For the "mental culture" of the early teachers was a group known as "The Mutual Improvement Society." Its work preceded that of the Wesley Guild.

One of the first to take up the Guild Movement

It was in 1895 that King Street became one of the first to take up the Wesley Guild Movement for Young People. The Guild meetings were of a devotional, cultural and social nature. Mr. Deans recalled that the church used to be crammed for Guild Rallies which were held in different churches of the district.

He remembered the Guild Football League, the Lawn Tennis Club at Peverell Park, Badminton in the Lecture Hall; whilst Louie Green recalled travelling in the ferry to Oreston to play hockey matches against other churches during Reverend Hall's time (1914-1924). Mrs. Payne enjoyed the debates which were held. In the 1914 Jubilee booklet a boating club is mentioned. The meetings continued until the blitz.

The Methodist Association of Youth Clubs was started in 1945, and King Street has run its own Youth Clubs at various times since that date. Mrs. Beatrice Egbert and Mr. Gerald Payne remembered being involved in the work of an 'Inters Club' for the younger age range shortly after the war. When Sister Nora became deaconess she developed a Youth Fellowship on a Friday night.

Scholars eligible for Sick Club

Formed in 1867, the first secretary of the Sick Club was Mr. W. Davey. All scholars were eligible for membership and the sum of 1 penny a week was paid to the fund, and in the case of illness 2 shillings a week was paid out. At the end of the year the amount paid in, less a small sum kept in reserve was paid back again to the members. This club was still thriving in the early decades of this century.

Juvenile Missionary Society

Started in the 1870's, the first secretary was Mr. F. Sellick. Today its work continues although the name has changed from Juvenile to Junior.

Millbay Mission School

Started in the 1880's the Millbay Mission was a branch of King Street School. It was situated at Edgecumbe Place Millbay. An undated piece of paper amongst the papers of Jack Adams gave these thoughts; "Just a small room in a block of buildings housing a large number of people and known at the time as 'The Rookery' but which had some very fine characters. The Sunday Evening services were conducted by a 'Mission Band' of King Street Young People divided into 3 Companies, A, B, and C, each under a 'Captain', and taking the service once in three weeks. This proved a wonderful training ground for speakers, prayer leaders, soloists etc."

It was then decided that something must be done for the children. Mr. W. H. Ackland, a teacher at King Street formed a school which ran with large numbers attending for many years. Junior and Senior Classes were held there, the Band of Hope and Girls' Club, and work for Foreign Missions.

For their anniversary services the Millbay School would use the larger premises at King Street. The mission was destroyed in the blitz. Mr. W. Daw, Mr. W. Sellick, and Mr. E. Payne were actively involved with the work until the blitz. Our present Millbay Room commemorates its work and witness.

The Brotherhood

This grew out of the Senior and Young Men's classes. It aimed: "To gather into fellowship and retain in the church the great mass of men who otherwise would be in many cases uninfluenced by Christian teaching." Meetings were held every Sunday in the early days and Miss Gwen Fugler recalled that in the first decade the Brotherhood had an orchestra of sixteen members.

The Sisterhood

Started in the early days of the church this devotional meeting met a social need for a group of largely young mothers, even providing a creche. This is no longer attached to the Sisterhood as the age range has changed. Today there are some 32 members on the roll.

Large Sunday School Choir

Formed in 1905 and led by Daddy Woodward, the choir competed for the first time in 1906 in the Plymouth and District Sunday School Union Eisteddford, and were placed 4th out of 10 choirs. By 1907 it had been placed first 6 times. In 1914 the choir had between 40 and 50 voices. This choir continued until some years before the war.

Daddy (Harry) Woodward also maintained a large senior choir. Louie Green remembered signing up as the 74th member in 1911, and Mr. Reg Stephens said that when he joined the choir in 1916 the limit for numbers was set at 104. Miss Gwen Fugler recalled a Sunday School Anniversary evening service around 1930 when 95 members out of 96 were present. Mr. Stephens also had a colourful memory of about twenty men of the Royal Artillery garrisoned in Plymouth sitting in the church in their brilliant scarlet uniforms. This was in the early years of the century when church attendance was compulsory for the soldiers.

Pleasant Sunday Afternoon

This was a Sunday afternoon meeting known for short as the P.S.A. Started during the time of Reverend Hall (1918-1924) it continued for many years with the involvement of Mr. and Mrs. Tink, until the late fifties.

Peter Pan in Wesley Hall in 1981.

10th Plymouth Company Boys' Brigade.

An interesting service took place in the Church after the evening service on Founder's Day, October 29th. A large number of the congregation remained behind to witness the annual Enrolment and Re-Enrolment Service of our Company of the Boys' Brigade. The Officer in Charge was Mr. S. G. Pester, who presented, first the four Officers, then the eight N.C.O's., and finally the thirty-three Privates for enrolment by the Chaplain, Rev. W. James Beckett, who handed to each his Membership Card for the new session. After the Brigade came the Life Boys, who had assembled independently of the Brigade, under their Lieutenant, Mr. L. Bond Spear, who presented twenty-two for enrolment.

October, 1933.

Pantomime Time

Three consecutive pantomimes were held in the Lecture Hall starting in 1945. This hall was the centre of all church activity after the loss of the other buildings. Ethel Williams told me that shows could last for some time and spanning a weekend which meant that everything had to be packed completely away so that Sunday Service could be held, and then set up again for the Monday performance. The profit went towards the rebuilding fund.

Mr. Payne also recalled Easter plays in earlier years and sketches performed by the choir in the evenings of the two day Bazaars, which for many years raised funds to help the work of the Deaconess.

Reviving the annual pantomime in 1971, Mr. Michael Mann has now produced eleven pantomimes, many written by Tony Raine. Profits from these have been given to the National Children's Home.

Formed in 1905, the Sunday School Choir; seen here with Daddy Woodward and the Challenge Banner which they won three years in succession (1907-1909).

The Sunday School Union procession in 1957, a few months before the opening of the new church.

Cradle Roll

This was established in 1909 by Miss Gladys Spear. Miss Esme Wragg told me how Miss Sally Almond would take layettes to Cradle Roll babies in the deprived area around King Street.

May Knox, Pam Maunder and now Esme Wragg, have looked after the cradle roll in more recent years, sending birthday cards, visiting if required and inviting parents and babies to Carol Services, Cradle Roll services, and Junior Church Anniversary services.

Brownies and Guides

This was thriving in the 30's and early 40's with the help of such people as Lizzie Stoneman and May Knox. Esme Wragg involved between 1936 and 1941 remembers times when there were 30 Brownies and 30 Guides. She recalled the poverty of those days when it was necessary to collect uniforms after a meeting for fear that they might otherwise be sold; the need to provide food for them and even a wash, trips out to Clearbrook and Plymbridge. The blitz brought an end to these activities.

Mr. Harper Recalls

In the early days lunchtime concerts were performed in the new building and Mr. Harper remembered that he returned to the church to collect some music on one occasion when he met a Mr. Ronald Thompson, who played him some complicated pieces from memory. He was subsequently invited to play the accompaniment for the Messiah at Christmas for the next twenty five years. He played also for each Easter performance of Olivet to Calvary or The Crucifixion.

The first full performance of the Messiah at Christmas was in December 1958.

In the early years King Street was able to provide all its own soloists for the performances on one occasion both the Reverends Harker and Hadfield were there to sing in a choir of 107 voices.

Wives' Club

A few years after the war a Thursday afternoon Wives' Club with creche was set up by Sister Edith Anstey, deaconess at the time. Gradually young families moved out, in the rebuilding of post-war Plymouth and numbers dwindled.

A Toddlers' Club started by Sister Nora Trineman in 1964 ran for some years on a Friday morning until the late seventies. After a lapse this has now been revived.

Fellowship Classes

Class Meetings were the original concept of John Wesley before the first Methodist Church was built, that small groups of up to twelve should meet for testimony. Mrs. Vera Spear recalled some classes who met for study, prayer and fellowship, which have been run this century. Leaders' names include Miss Mitchell, Miss Lillie Stoneman, Mrs. Stella Payne, Miss Louie Green, Sister Nora, and herself Vera Spear.

She remembered that regular prayer meetings were held, out of which the Thursday morning Bible Class evolved.

A Deaconess Remembers

King Street had a deaconess working with them before the Order of Deaconesses was formed.

Sister Nora Trineman took up her post as Deaconess in 1951, living in a house at Warleigh Road and eventually in the flat at Asbury House. She spent eight years working at King Street; her work stretching across all aspects of church life, and she gave me a picture of "an after the war dullness" — not the extreme poverty of the twenties and thirties, but of deprivation amongst the rubble of war.

She remembered large old houses around the original church, divided into flats and packed with people; giving gifts of clothing to various families only to hear that they had been sold, and one particular family who were known for their attempts to set fire to things, including King Street Church!

She remembered the Sunday School picnics held for many years at Bere Ferrers and in 1958 a Girls' Brigade camp at Paignton.

The Girls' Brigade

Started by Sister Nora Trineman in 1957 this ran for a few years. It was known as the 12th Plymouth Company and had up to 20 older girls and 10 little ones.

The Friendship Club

This was developed when the new church was built, run at the time by Mr. and Mrs. Robin. It was an afternoon club encouraging people not usually attenders at church, and organizing holidays to places like Southsea and Scarborough.

Mrs. Vera Spear remembered Mr. and Mrs. Ash who continued the work. Mr. Ash would give out small surprise packages to the winners of lucky numbers stuck under chairs, and his wife would bake large quantities of scones for their teas. Membership went up to about ninety at one time.

Until recently, Mr. and Mrs. Baron have been running the club.

Charity Work

In 1970, Edna and Bert Harper, Joan Weeks and Adrienne Buckler organised collections for a Guide Dog for the blind. At the time a Guide Dog cost £250. In 1986 it costs £1000 to train a dog and nearly enough for the sixth dog has been raised.

Boxes for the National Children's Home have been issued for many years, collections organised for over twenty years by Mrs. Edna Harper and recently taken over by Mrs. Pat Rowden. Pantomime profits have been sent to the fund also.

Christian Aid week collections and collections for foreign aid have been in the hands of Mrs. Mary Bolt since 1961.

INTO THE EIGHTIES

What's New in the last few years?

Clifford Bell and his wife Gladys were at King Street as the church entered the eighties, having introduced in their time a church family picnic which was held at alternative sites such as Wotter and Lee Moor after a Sunday morning service in June, and the custom of having church lunches on a regular basis, produced on by a team of helpers. Mrs. Beaulah Mann told me that they catered for about sixty people and eighty at Christmas.

In September 1981, Reverend Peter Bolt and his wife Joan took up their work at King Street. As well as the spiritual ministry, established clubs, house groups and special events continued and new ones were introduced (Michael and Beaulah Mann started their house fellowship in 1982).

The Junior Church plant bulbs in autumn 1981.

The Youth Choir, Plymouth Praisemakers started by Reverend Bolt drew in young people from circuit churches also and gave its first performance at Christmas 1981. They have since given regular performances and undertaken short tours at Easter and in August. A Youth Fellowship started meetings after evening service in Autumn 1981 and the Youth Club which was re-established after a lapse of some time became known as the Hutt Club and has been operating intermittently on a Friday evening. A junior section of the youth choir, Junior Praise, was established by Michael Chown for 9—13 year olds in 1984 meeting after Junior Church. They regularly give a musical contribution to morning worship.

Youth and Community worker Debbie Wolters arrived from America in January 1982 of six months. She set up a junior club, the Shell Group which ran for some months. She was followed in September 1982 by another American, Rock Jones who also worked for Youth and Community until June 1983. The following October his father Reverend Frank Jones came from America to conduct a mission aimed specifically at the neighbourhood. A Craft Festival took place at the same time.

Also in 1984 a Day of Fellowship replaced the church picnic; a meal after morning service followed by discussion groups. Similar Days of Fellowship have been held since. August 1984 saw the visit of the Rev. Charles Turkington and his wife, from America. A considerable sum of money was raised to aid the Ethiopean disaster fund in 1984, organised by Mrs. Mary Bolt.

In 1983, Meeting Point evolved out of what had previously been known as the Tuesday Club, an interest club, which itself had been developed from a Wives' Club. Rev. Bolt ran a monthly Bible Study. A Men's Supper Club was also started in 1983.

The Plymouth Praisemakers with the Rev. Peter Bolt and Rev. Amos Cresswell in 1984.

Hunger lunches whose profits went to charities were introduced in Lent 1985, by Beaulah Mann and Pat Rowden, following the Thursday Prayer Fellowship.

Also established in 1984 was a Thursday Wives' Club by Elizabeth Wright, a Music Workshop by Reverend Peter Bolt which worked with and augmented the choir in musical items on special occasions, a Flower Guild by Mrs. James and Mrs. Hortop prior to which there had been a Sunday evening flower distribution for many years, and a Book Counter by Tony Raine.

King Street and St. Andrews Church have combined for evening services for the last couple of years, thus realising the hope mentioned at the re-building of the church in 1957 that there should be links between the two churches.

In 1985 a Mother and Toddler club was started on a Friday by Elizabeth Wright and Pat Rowden. A little used room was prepared as a new creche for Sundays. Recently, a monthly Prayer Fellowship has been started on a Monday night at the Manse.

Age Concern who had used the premises for their meetings and for meals had their own buildings completed nearby and moved out in the early eighties. The College of Further Education also ended their use of the premises which they had used for some years, but a Language school and Weight Watchers will continue to do so. In 1986 a gymnastics club called Tumble Tots have started using the premises.

Circuit re-organization over the years

The Plymouth Circuits

1783 Plymouth Circuit formed.
1794 Launceston Circuit formed from Plymouth.
1795 Plymouth Circuit called Plymouth Dock Circuit.
1813 Plymouth Dock Circuit divides into Plymouth and Plymouth Dock.
1871 Plymouth divides into King Street and Ebenezer.
1934 Ebenezer unites with the ex-Methodist Greenbank. Ex-Primitive Methodist Cobourg Street and ex-U.M. Ebrington Street joined to King Street. Ex-Wesleyan and ex-U.M. Devonport Circuits unite.
1940 The Plymouth and Devonport circuits unite.
1944 Plymouth and Devonport Mission formed.
1945 Plymouth East divides from King Street-and-Devonport.
1952 King Street and Devonport divide.
1973 Plymouth Methodist Circuit is formed.
1977 Some members from Mutley join King Street after the closure of Mutley church.

King Street Ministers

Rev. William Maltby	1892-1895	Rev. W. J. Beckett	1933-1936
Rev. J. C. Sowerbutts	1895-1898	Rev. W. E. Woodall	1936-1940
Rev. Thomas Rippon	1898-1901	Rev. F. A. Hickling	1940-1946
Rev. E. D. Dannatt	1901-1904	Rev. F. C. Crump	1946-1950
Rev. W. J. Burrow	1904-1907	Rev. F. A. Rowe	1950-1956
Rev. J. W. Britton	1907-1910	Rev. R. E. Grose	1956-1958
Rev. John Kinnings	1910-1913	Rev. A. R. Martin	1958-1959
Rev. H. C. Morton	1913-1918	Rev. M. Harker	1959-1966
Rev. A. F. Hall	1918-1924	Rev. D. Hadfield	1966-1975
Rev. G. E. Mitchell	1924-1927	Rev. C. Bell	1975-1981
Rev. E. Calvert	1927-1929	Rev. P. Bolt	1981-
Rev. G. L. Robinson	1929-1933		

As I looked at the story of King Street I felt very much aware of the dedicated service that so many people had given over the years; a feeling of the church's roots and a sense of continuity.

Initially I thought how appropriate it would be to mention all the leaders and workers of the different sections of the church as it is today. Rapidly I became aware that the people who give freely of their time and energy at present are numerous and many others who are still members have been actively involved in work until quite recently. It seemed impossible to include every person. I therefore decided to include names where they formed part of the story. I have also become very much aware of the length of service which many people have given to a particular aspect of church life. It has been quite common for someone to tell me that they have led an organisation for over twenty years.

Many people have given me of their time and memories, willingly answering my questions, telling anecdotes, checking details, loaning photographs, plans, and so on. To these people I am indebted: Mrs. Marion Adams, Mrs. Joan (Darey) Bolt, Mrs. Mary Bolt, Rev. Peter Bolt, Mr. Gerald Bowden, Mrs. Pat Bowden, Mrs. Peggy Brimmell, Mrs. Ella Cooke, Mr. Michael Cooke, Mrs. Barbara Chown, Mr. Michael Chown, Mr. Arthur Clamp, Mrs. Gwen Darey, Mr. Harry Deans, Mr. John Edmondson, Mrs. Beatrice Egbert, Miss Gwen Fugler, Miss Muriel Goad, Miss Louie Green, Mrs. Mollie Hadfield, Mr. Bertram Harper, Mrs. Edna Harper, Mrs. Betty Hortop, Mr. Fred Hortop, Mrs. Pam Maunder, Mrs. Beaulah Mann, Mr. Michael Mann, Mr. Gerald Payne, Mrs. Stella Payne, Rev. Fred Raine, Mr. Tony Raine, Mr. John Rowden, Mrs. Pat Rowden, Mr. Brian Spear, Mrs. Vera Spear, Mr. Reg Stephens, Sister Nora Trineman, The Western Morning News, Mrs. Ethel Williams, Miss Esme Wragg, Mrs. Elizabeth Wright, Mr. Paul Wright.

I have also had access to photos, documents, etc. belonging to the late Mr. Jack Adams, Mrs. Kell and Mr. L. B. Spear.

Documents included the Sunday School Jubilee Booket of 1910, the Souvenir Programme of the opening of the new building in 1957, Newspaper cuttings of the Western Morning News and Evening Herald, Conference Handbooks, and the Methodist Recorder.

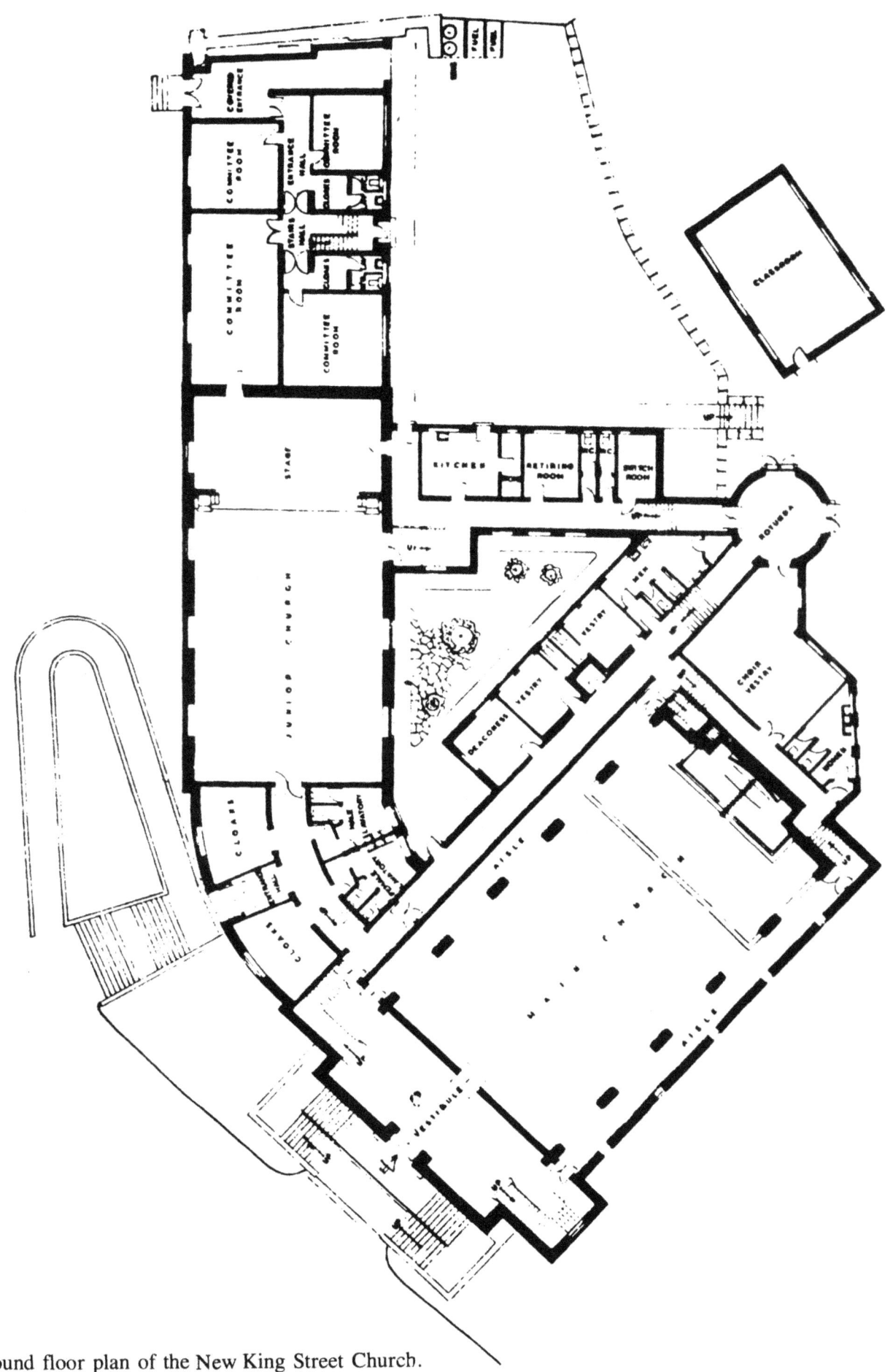

Ground floor plan of the New King Street Church.

Some of the congregation on July 6th, 1986. Rev. Amos Cresswell led the services. Thirty years ago, on July 18th, 1956, the foundation stone was laid here. *Photo: Peter McMullin.*

Arthur L. Clamp – the man behind the books

Arthur Leslie Clamp was a man of boundless energy with a passion for helping others, particularly through his love of history. A printer by trade, he started his career in a printing company before moving his family from Exeter to Plymouth to teach at the Plymouth College of Art and Design, where he eventually became the Head of the Printing Department.

Arthur with his five children.

A Devoted Family Man

Despite his love of teaching, Arthur prioritised his family, always making it home by 5:30pm for tea. He and his wife, Rosemary, raised five children: Susan, Angela, Elizabeth, David, and Steven. Arthur would often combine his love of family and history by taking his children on Sunday walks, encouraging them to appreciate historical monuments by taking photos or making crayon rubbings of gravestones for his books. The family home at 203 Elburton Road was a hub of activity, with a large garden, featuring a two-storey fort and a makeshift swimming pool.

A Lifelong Learner and Adventurer

Arthur's thirst for knowledge extended beyond history to a deep curiosity about the world. He was passionate about exploring different cultures, traditions, and cuisines, often taking advantage of his long summer holidays as a teacher to travel to places like India, Russia, South America, the middle east and the USA, sometimes bringing one of his children along. This adventurous spirit even influenced his home life, as seen by the short-lived family tradition of steam-cooking vegetables after a trip to Iceland.

History is a prominent feature of family days out

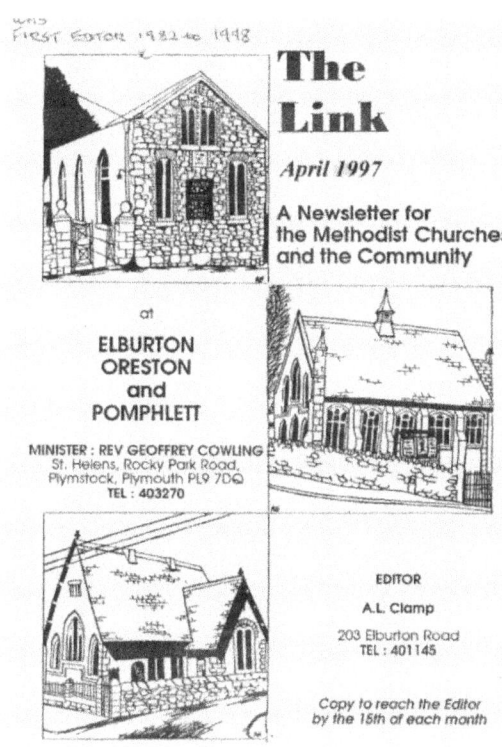

Community and Philanthropic Spirit

His commitment to serving others was evident in his long-standing involvement with the Elburton Methodist Church. He was the Sunday School Superintendent for over 15 years and served as the editor of the wider church's monthly newsletter, "The Link," for a similar duration. After Rosemary's very sad passing, Arthur later remarried and, following a chance encounter with a professor from India, established a connection with a missionary school in Chennai. Together with his new wife, Christine, he co-founded a "Sponsor a Child's Education" program that continues to this day.

Pictured left – The cover of 'The Link' complete with hand drawn sketches of each church by Angela
Below right – Arthur Clamp promoting his latest book
Below left – Arthur at home with his first wife, Rosemary
Below centre – Arthur on holiday with his second wife, Christine

A Legacy of Learning and Positivity

Arthur's greatest passion was history, which he brought to life through tireless research, documentation, and the many books he authored. He was driven by a need to "never be stuck in a rut," constantly seeking new experiences, meeting new people, and expanding his knowledge. With a positive attitude and a great sense of humour, he was always ready to help others, leaving a lasting impact on his family and community. His children, Susan, Angela, Elizabeth, David, and Steven, remember him with love and gratitude.

David Clamp, 2025

A Legacy of Local History

Below is the story of how Arthur L Clamp began writing books, in his own words, drafted shortly before he passed away in 2001. I have only made minor alterations to this text, correcting grammatical errors that he did not survive to correct himself. When I first discovered this text, I was shocked to see my name mentioned. It seems that, unbeknownst to me, I shared my first PC with him. I suspect he used it during the day when I was at school, although I do have one memory of sitting with him and showing him how it worked. It has been a pleasure to pick up where he left off and see his books republished and redistributed, and to know that I was part of the story, even back then. It was also fascinating to discover that his pricing structure matches the way I have tried to price the books, with a third going to local sellers and the rest covering printing costs with a little left over for my expenses.

I am his eldest grandson, and it is a privilege to curate his legacy, which we are calling 'The Clamp Collection'. The very last line of the text originally reads "The following pages list all the titles." Sadly, that page is missing and we have no record of all the books he published and knowing that some of those were researched by other authors makes the process of finding them even harder. I look forward to one day completing the collection and seeing them all available again. And maybe, one day, I'll even start writing my own to add to the series. For now, here is his story in his own words.

Steven Gibson, 2025

Writing and Publishing Booklets on Local Topics and Areas

I started this interest in either 1968 or 1969 when living in Woodford. I had by these dates established the Department of Printing and I think I must have been looking for something different to do. The first titles were of A5 size proofed from type set at Clarke, Doble and Brendon, Ltd., Plymouth printers, and then made up into pages and printed at Sawtell and Neilson, Ltd., Totnes.

Then began a slow process of getting them out to shops, etc. which proved to be more time consuming and difficult than actually researching, writing and getting the books into print. However, I persisted and opened a business account with Barclays Bank on the Broadway. I was advised to give it a title so I called it "Westway Publications". There came along another problem, one of storage of paper and finished books which was solved when the family moved to Elburton in 1970.

I changed the printer to Penwell, Ltd., Callington, Cornwall, as he was then just setting up himself and his prices seemed very reasonable. I did not get any of the printers to make up the complete books. I hand folded the flat printed sheets, stitched the books on a small manual table stitcher and trimmed them in a small hand turned guillotine which I bought from someone in Penzance for £40. It was brought up in a van.

The trouble and time going to and fro to Callington was too much so I transferred the printing to PDS Printers, Prince Rock, Plymouth, and I have been with them ever since. Now they are at Plympton which is easy to reach and they fold the flat sheets which was turning out to be a long chore which only saved a small part of the printing costs.

All my first titles were written by myself. I took the photographs and developed them in the loft of the house, the type was set by now on a computer situated in the house at Elburton from which I had collected photographic lengths of text to cut up and law down as pages.

At some point I decided that I would do my own film processing of lith film so I bought a large second hand process camera from Kingsbridge and learnt through trial and error to make line negatives of the text and halftone negatives of the illustrations which proved more difficult than I anticipated. The main problem was trying to keep the developer in the large dish at the correct temperature as any change would affect the developing time. I replaced this old camera with a brand new one bought from Croydon, Surrey, costing £900. This has turned out to be a great asset cutting out an expensive part of the printer's costs and one crucial aspect of the work which I could control.

By the middle 1970s there were many outlets I had contacted in Plymouth, up to Dartmoor, Exeter, around to Torbay, Totnes, Dartmouth and the South Hams. The market for local books was much greater than I had first thought and through getting to know many local people undertaking research themselves had the chance to help and make up books for other people who had in most instances, got together a collection of photographs with some text in a rather muddled way. Through my experience in print I was able to shape up their work and get it into print and in every case I had to pay the printer and let the person have the royalties. In the majority of titles produced in this manner this was another way of producing titles and it did give some profit to my work. However, I must say that in a few cases I lost out by either the other person getting the numbers wrong, not returning any monies from stock I delivered or they thought that more of their books should have been sold.

The print run was usually 1,000 copies and from time to time I have had reprints of 250 copies. It took about ten years to clear the first print run so I always had large stocks in the garage, workshop, etc. The numbers sold during the early years was about 7,000 copies a year increasing to around 9,000 copies and for the whole of the enterprise about 500,000 have been sold. The booklets have become part of the local scene and many people collect them, shops regularly order copies and I go around certain areas month by month restocking or replacing titles as necessary.

During the past year or so I have started setting the text on a Packard Bell PC, something which I should have done some years back. I share it with Steven Gibson, my grandson. There appears to be no end to the market for local books, but I could not earn a regular income because of the long time it takes to sell stock.

However, now exceeding 100 titles made up mainly of A4 twenty-four page booklets, some folded guides, with selling prices set with a third going to the shop which is the trade custom, the original idea has been quite successful and could go on for ever.

Apart from monetary benefits, however spasmodically these might be, I have learnt a lot myself, met many interesting people and have become part of the local scene with requests to give talks and to advise people about getting into print.

Arthur L Clamp, 2001

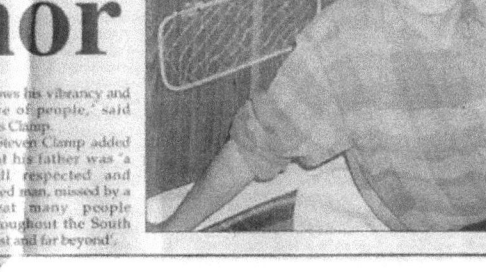

This newspaper article, published by the Evening Herald on 17th August 2001, forms a good record of his life. Just as he encourages us to learn more about local history, we encourage you to learn a little about him. For that reason, we have included these pages at the back of all the most recently republished books, in honour of his memory and recognition of his contribution to the community.